Cover Art: Pharaoh Laboa
Content and Stories: Various Ghosts

Does your story need to be heard?
Send Email to: exposeTHEelephant@gmail.com.

Content Advisory: This book is intended for mature audiences and contains graphic violence, explicit sexual activity and disturbing imagery.

Content, Stories, Art, Illustrations and other fun stuff: © StrateQuest Publishing, stratequestpublishing@gmail.com, contributed as personal stories by authors that wish to remain anonymous.

Copyright © 2020 by StrateQuest Publishing

No part of this publication may be reproduced, stored in a retrieval system, or transmitted in any form or by any means, media, electronic, internet, screen, stage, script, conversation, mechanical, photocopying, recording, scanning, videography, social media, or otherwise, except as permitted under Section 107 of 108 of the 1976 United States Copyright Act, without the prior written permission of the publisher, author or trustees.

Limit of Liability/Disclaimer of Warranty: While the publisher, author, ghost authors and artists have used their best efforts in preparing this book, they make no representations or warranties about the subject matter, the accuracy or completeness of the contents of this book and specifically disclaim any implied warranty, merchantability, use or fitness for a particular purpose. The stories herein do not contain advice or recommendations and any of the content may not be suitable for your situation. Neither the publisher, the author, the ghost authors or artists shall be liable for damages arising herefrom.

ISBN: 978-0-9822570-8-1

More stories from the

· MORE STORIES FROM THE ·

#exposeTHEelephant

Thanks to:

My Boys ~ I Love You, I will

#ALWAYSLoveYOU ~Dada

My mother / My father

Sisters / Brothers

Friends / Colleagues

The Ghostwriters

The Jokewriters

The Comedians

The Musicians

The Artists

Note:

The stories in this book are gruesomely true. Any resemblance to your story; however, is simply just coincidence, just know that you're not alone.

If there is any small inkling of resemblance, I'm sorry you had to go through that.

If you are still out there suffering in silence, my prayer is that you will find your path.

Contents

Lasso my Asso 1

It takes a Village, People.... 35

George Adam Yellow............ 65

Fill my Purpose 89

Roses are Red Violet be Cra Cra 117

More stories from the

#trueSTORY

Lasso my Asso

Ciara rose slowly from their bed feeling like she'd taken a beating.

"Hope rises" is the theme the priest kept repeating during the sermon message in church yesterday.

Ciara thought "Hope does not rise, it drowns."

The pretty, petite, 32 year old had given up hope many years ago.

After marrying her childhood sweetheart, Jared, an unlucky 13 years ago she was gradually separated from her family, her friends, her job, and her bank account.

At first Jared would say "You are my Princess! I am made to worship you, there's no reason for you to have so much focus on (insert whatever was important to Ciara from her previous life) all we need is each other!"

To a young girl that idea had a rather romantic feel about it. Ciara first thought she should feel grateful, pampered, cherished.

And she did. Until the punching started.

As she rose out of bed this morning she felt like she'd taken a beating because she had.

After church Jared started drinking his Jack Daniels. He only allowed himself to drink on Sundays after church. Embarking on some of that, you know, "controlled drinking". But, his binge drinking always reaches epic proportions and he's a very mean drunk.

The beatings were not directly related to alcohol, or Sundays. They could happen any time of any day of the week.

By the time the physical abuse started Jared had already severed any of the lifelines that might have allowed Ciara to leave when it became literally painful to stay in the marriage. The abuse by a Narcissistic Sociopath is low and slow. Victims never see it coming.

"Your mother always judges me, I work hard, why do I have to put up with her shit?" Jared would say as an excuse not to see her family.

Ciara had to admit her mother had always been wary of, and icy toward, Jared.

Mother knows best and that woman just happened to be 100% on the bullseye.

"You're married now "mi amore", no reason to go out with Nancy and Jackie. They're sluts, you're an angel. What do you expect me to think when you go out with them when you could be home with me?" Jared would say to block his wife from seeing her friends until they just gave up trying to get together with her.

Jared was absolute from the moment of the engagement that he'd bring in the paycheck, Ciara would tend the home and children. Sounded fair to the new Mrs. Holder. In the Holder's culture, the man is the breadwinner and the wife stays home. The way the Bible intended it.

"Man" because after marriage he's still his own man and "wife" because after marriage she's property.

The one place Ciara was allowed to go was to their local Catholic church.

To better fit in with the many, many, evangelicals and baptists in the area the Sacred Heart Church worked within a Wednesday evening, and Sunday morning, schedule.

Ciara tried whenever she could to come to any task with a servant's heart. Food drives, quilting circles, bake sales, tending to the homebound members, working in the nursery, Ciara never said no.

While it felt a little like freedom it was actually the one place Jared could feel completely confident about allowing his wife to go alone. He even insisted on going to the grocery store and hair salon visits with her so she had no need to touch money or their credit cards.

Yet, even at church, Ciara wasn't safe from Jared's abuse.

"That ass! Just look! Ciara, your ass is getting wider every day since I married you!" Jared would yell across the Fellowship Hall just as she was bending over to clear some plates after the shared luncheon. All of the husbands would laugh. These insults would be held back quietly until the priest left the immediate vicinity.

As if that made it alright.

The wives and kids would keep their eyes down and mostly Ciara was allowed to go on with the rest of the event, unnoticed.

Whether the arrangement was formal or just how things had always been, the women were never left without a couple of male minders.

They'd become accustomed to the idea that the men were there to protect, to shield, to help.

Ciara fully realized one moment too late that what she really needed protection from was her husband.

****

"Ciara! Top off my drink and bring me a new pack of cigarettes." Jared bellowed.

It had been two weeks since the last Sunday nights beating, with a few slaps across the face or punch to the lower back sprinkled in.

"Bitch, get out here right now before I thump you!" Jared yelled.

Thinking to himself, "Maybe this time I'll use my highball glass to thump her instead of just my fist. Stupid cow."

Early in the marriage Jerad adopted the strategy of only hitting Ciara on the top of the head, or the base of her skull, or just above her ears. That way the bruises didn't show beneath her long, glossy, black hair.

The rest of the bruises could be covered by modest clothing befitting any good wife.

"Finally!" Jared said, shaking his head, as Ciara approached with his bottle and smokes.

Without another word, he held out the glass in his hand for a refill and his other hand for the cigarettes and lighter.

"Come on, sit down with me wifey." Cooed Jared.

Ciara sat.

"Honey," said Jared leaning in toward Ciara causing her to

flinch although Jerad didn't even notice "Look, the boss has been on my ass. I am working like crazy for us. If you could just try to think about me and what I need when I'm stressed then I wouldn't... boil over like I do sometimes. Understand?"

"Yes, of course, my darling. I know you work hard, I'll try harder." offering him her best smile even as the hairs on the back of her neck and forearms began to rise.

Hope rises.

That's total bullshit.

"Baby, I'm going to go finish the dishes, do you want to have a shower before bed?" ventured Ciara.

"No you stupid, fat, cunt I do not want a shower before bed." whining the final words to mock his wife. It was hard to tell if the alcohol was talking or if it was Jared.

He loved calling Ciara fat when in fact, her wedding dress

was now a little baggy on her 13 years after the ceremony. Jareds constant bagging on her caused her self image to cave to the point of unhealthy weight loss.

The children never came. Ciara could conceive but she endured three miscarriages before the doctor pronounced her completely barren.

Jared blamed her. Neither Ciara nor the doctor told him the severe beatings likely dislodged and killed the baby within her womb. Three babies. Ciara only wished she were in fact "fat" from carrying and having those lost little angels.

Ciara recognized the ugly words and profanity from Jared at this moment were her cue to exit stage right leaving the bottle and the cigarettes with her abusive husband.

She set into washing dishes when she noticed Jared was no longer sitting by the firepit, the bottle wasn't there, either.

"Oh, God have mercy," Ciara whispered, grasping the crucifix around her neck and kissing Jesus' feet.

When Jared got drunk and went for a walkabout, very bad things happened.

Ciara kept washing and watching, on heightened alert.

About thirty minutes later Jared came in through the front door, with a lit cigarette in his mouth and clutching the now mostly empty Jack Daniels bottle.

"NOW, I'vemm ready for my shouter. My showler... my shower!" Jared finally managed to slur out.

Ciara concentrated on drying the pot she just washed with the same intensity she imagined it took to split atoms. Nodding politely and keeping her eyes downcast.

"Ok honey, you enjoy!" She glanced up just long enough to deliver her words with a smile.

"Oh!" Ciara gasped as she saw Jared had shifted his cigarette into his left hand and as he was leaning against the living room wall for support he was burning a hole in the quilt her grandmother made to celebrate her launch into wedded bliss.

"Yaya's quilt! Jared, step away!" cried Ciara.

Losing her beloved Grandmother a year after her wedding was the hardest thing Ciara had ever endured and that includes Jared's beatings.

Her grandmother was truly an angel. Yaya knew everything and could heal anything. And now, Ciara's most prized possession connecting her to Yaya was defiled by her husband's filthy cigarette.

"What did you say to me?" Jared glowered.

"Please, please Jared just move over here I'll get you some water. You know we both love Yaya's quilt!" Ciara pleaded.

"You fucking BITCH!" Jared yelled as he turned and in one motion pulled the quilt down off the wall and carried it to the firepit where he threw it into the flames.

Ciara tried to pull it out, even if she could only save one square that Yaya's beautiful hands had created just for her. That wasn't part of Jared's plan, though. He held her tight with her arms bound to her sides as she quietly cried, watching the last piece of Yaya burn to death before her very eyes.

When the cotton and stuffing had burned to ashes Jared let Ciara go. She sank to the ground in front of the embers.

"That's it." Ciara said. So softly Jared at first thought he must have imagined it and kept walking. Just before reaching the back door he heard Ciara roar "No more, Jared! No more!" As he turned, Jared realized Ciara had picked up a short, thick, branch from the woodpile and looked like she meant to hit him with it.

This confused Jared's drunken brain for about three seconds.

If Ciara hadn't waited two seconds to swing she might still be alive today.

Jared grabbed the branch mid-swing and easily ripped it out of his wife's hands as she shouted and cried "You take everything I love and destroy it! I'm leaving! I'm leaving tonight and I want a divorce!"

Jared went suddenly still. Ciara thought it must be what Lot's wife looked like when she took a final, forbidden glance at Sodom before turning into a pillar of salt.

She was in shock, he was in shock, then she was headed into the house for the truck keys, and just as she reached for them on the peg by the door she was toppled to the ground. He'd hit her on the back of both knees with the thick branch, the wind knocked out of her in her fall.

Ciara lies opening and closing her mouth like a mackerel left out of water on the dock.

She still couldn't quite breathe when the first blinding shock hit. "When did he get a taser?" Ciara wondered until that thought was eclipsed by Jared's face.

He leaned closer into Ciara's face "You. Are. NOT. Going. ANYWHERE! Ever."

The way he said "Ever" so calmly and quietly let Ciara know she'd either have to escape or he'd finally finish her.

Just as she thought she could gather up enough strength to rise like the elusive hope, Jared kicked her over and again shocked her with the taser's current, this time on her flat belly.

If the electrical currents had knocked Ciara completely out it would have been a mercy.

Instead, she felt herself being dragged into an area in the

big work barn where Jared kept his precious Ford F150 pickup truck.

Jared got a big duffle bag out of the second-row seating of the tall truck. Something Ciara had never seen before.

"This here's my 'divorce prevention kit' wifey. I'm like a fucking boyscout, always prepared!" Jared said with a sick smile.

Ciara's head was swimming from the blow, the fall then the tazing but her mind went crystal clear very quickly as she watched Jerad pull a noose out of the bag.

"Oh, no, oh please God, no." Ciara whispered.

"God isn't here Ciara! Not for you!" Jared said in a nearly emotionless voice as he advanced on her.

She tried to crawl away but using the noose like a lasso Jared expertly swung the rope around Ciara's neck pulling it taught.

She tried to claw the noose away from her neck. She only managed to snap the chain holding her crucifix and as she breathed in dust and cried she looked at Jesus, face down in the dirt and nailed to the cross. The perfect, blameless, victim and she was sure she was about to meet him face-to-face.

Next Jared bound Ciara's ankles together then proceeded to tie the longer end of the rope to the trailer hitch mounted on the back bumper of his truck.

He chatted as he worked "See, mi amore, I've always known you had a feisty streak. Knew it in high school and knew it ever since the blessed day of our wedding. I thought I'd mostly thumped it out of your stupid brain but, here we are! Jared making a sick and crazy-eyed motion like Jack Nicholson poking his head through a hole in a door. You're not leaving me, you're not divorcing me, I'm tired of your bullshit and having to watch you all the time." Narcissists never see their part.

"No!" Ciara begged "Jared please no. I won't leave, I promise. You know I'd never divorce you! I'll be good. I'll be good, please just untie me! I'll forget this whole night!"

With a reptilian gleam in his eyes, Jared just said through a smile "No you won't."

Then he got in the big truck, started up the engine, and began driving out of the barn toward the county road in front of their marital home, watching with a sick grin the rear camera.

As Ciara tried to grasp at anything she could hold on to, to make this all stop the only thing she managed to grab was her crucifix and it wasn't nearly strong enough to save her.

Once at the road Jared turned on his signal indicating they were going north on the road, away from town.

"I wonder why he's using his turn signal?" Ciara mused

just before the truck accelerated, dragging her over rocks and asphalt.

She screamed, she cried, she tried to shield her body and head from the abuse, she begged for mercy from Jared and from God but no one answered.

Near a grove of pecan trees Ciara knew to be a half a mile away from their home Jared pulled over and stopped.

He jumped out of the truck and while walking toward her said "Enjoying our little late-night ride??"

Ciara could only whimper "No more, please Jared no more."

He laughed in her face and got back into the truck. Knowing it was truly ride or die time Ciara scrambled to a hands and knees position. Kneeling up briefly to try and get the noose loose enough to at least let her breathe when Jared spotted her in the vehicle's rear camera.

She only heard "Bitch!" then felt a thump as he backed the truck into her, fast.

When she woke up, it could have been two minutes, it could have been two hours but judging by the maniacal look on Jared's face he was pissed she'd kept him waiting.

"Why Ciara? Why? I did everything for you, even paying for that fancy hair salon you insist on going to twice a month!"

Ciara decided now was not the time to explain the difference between a hair salon and Super Cuts. Plus she felt she was going in and out of consciousness.

"I'm sorry Jared, please take me home. Please, please, let me live!"

"If I do, there'll be no more wasting money on this hair!" he said as he yanked a big, matted, handful of her waist-long hair above her head. Ciara could see blood and dirt and straw in it.

"Never again," Ciara cried "I'll never go there or anywhere else you tell me not to, ever again!"

"I think I know how to make sure of that my little squaw." Ciara flinched at the ugly slur. She wasn't Native American herself but she'd be at the receiving end of some racist taunt or other her entire life.

Racism became the least of her worries when Jared opened his "divorce prevention kit", again, and got out his Gerber Gator fixed-blade hunting knife.

Whatever blood that hadn't come out along the bumpy road now drained from Ciara's face and pooled somewhere around her belly and she peed herself out of terror.

"Damn it, Ciara, what are you a little baby?!?!?! Pissing all over yourself? I gotta find more privacy to deal with you little squaw."

Ciara could only stare up through unblinking eyes at the cloudless night sky dotted with brilliant stars. Wondering, "Where is God?"

Jared slowly inched his truck into the pecan grove where their privacy was assured. Ciara noticed he was driving very slowly and carefully. She knew that wasn't for her. It was to make sure no stray branches scratched the red paint on his prized truck.

Then he was coming back at her and they both spotted the same thing at the same time. A dent in the back bumper where Jared hit Ciara and it had a clump of her hair stuck in it.

"MOTHER FUCKER!" Jared screamed in all-out rage. "Look what you fucking did!."

Ciara had no more "I'm Sorrys" left. Only fear. And it was growing.

Jared hauled her up into the bed of the truck, put a foot at the base of the noose around her neck, and began hacking away at her hair. Sometimes pulling it out in big clumps and sometimes cutting it away along with bits of her scalp. It was excruciating but Ciara could only cry softly.

She looked into his eyes as her own blood ran into her eyes making the stars in the sky turn bright pink in her vision. "Jared, rot in hell, you sick fat bastard."

Jared kicked Ciara's body off of the truck bed back onto the dirt, got into the cab of his truck, and drove at high speeds both on straightaways and into turns. It's difficult to say exactly when the life force completely left Ciara's body. At one point she noted the large "Frank's Family Dairy" farm, meaning they were two miles from home.

She died thinking how Jared never did like to drive at night and this was such a long way around the county.

That, and how Jesus' flesh was pierced and flayed. How

he died so horribly. To save us from our sins. "Why wasn't I worth saving?" Ciara whispered as she let the crucifix drop out of her hand.

＊＊＊＊＊＊＊＊＊＊

"Hey Carl we've got a mess up here on Route 19, looks like someone hit another deer." Deputy Larson let up on the radio button so the weekday dispatcher Carl could acknowledge he received the information.

"Alright, I'll get Irwin out there with the truck to haul it off before the kids see it from the school bus on the way this morning. Happy Monday, buddy! Out."

Chuckling Larson replied "You, too buddy. You, too."

It was a glorious sunrise. Deputy Larson appreciated it while again wondering why deer refused to use headlights. Or at least stay tucked in a copse of trees at dusk and dawn when so many of them meet their maker launched from someone's front bumper or windshield.

At the same time dispatcher Carl took a smoke break to also admire the sunrise.

That swaggering sack of shit Jared Holder was heading his way.

"Howdy Carl, how's it hanging?"

"Just fine Jared. Hey, what's all that blood from?"

Jared looked at his hands like he'd never seen them before in his life. "Had to break up a dog fight. Not my blood." and offered one of those shit-eating grins he is so famous for, at least to Carl.

Jared lit one up indicating he wasn't moving away fast or very soon then said "So what's up in your detective world these days?" and gave a chuckle. Like he'd hit high comedy by pointing out Carl wasn't a real police officer but only a desk jockey dispatcher.

"Aw, nothing," Carl replied "Just someone hit a deer up on Route 19. Getting the cleaning crew out now before the school kids see it. Deputy Larson made it sound like it's real bad."

As he finished his sentence Carl turned to look at Jerad who was nowhere to be seen. "Crazy sum'bitch." Carl murmured as he crushed out his cigarette.

Deputy Larson was stretching his back wondering how long the truck with the winch on the back would take to come clear the animal away. He was feeling hungry for his favorite sunny side up eggs with whole wheat toast and at least four more cups of black coffee when something caught his eye.

In the brightening morning sun, he saw something that, while the color of a deer pelt, looked decidedly manmade.

He walked a few feet from the front of his patrol car to the object lying just on the side of the road in a shallow ditch.

He covered his mouth but his words still escaped "Holy Christ on a cracker what in the actual fuck?"

He walked around trying to convince himself it was still a deer. "Still a deer, it's just a deer." But there was no arguing this was a woman. Or at least the bits and tatters left of a small woman hardly recognizable.

He jumped back on the mic "Carl, get the Sheriff and the medical examiner here right away. Keep this as quiet as you can, we have a Signal 30 up here and I don't want an audience gathering."

"Really?!" Carl said excitedly

"Yes, really Carl now do as I tell you, and do it quick." said Larson in a tone that told Carl to act like a professional.

"Oh, yeah, sorry, yeah... call out the Sheriff and M.E. but otherwise keep it quiet. I'm on it. Deputy Larson, what about the school bus?"

"Shit" said Larson looking up the road for any sign of something shiny and yellow.

By leaning two rifles against two trees and hanging a tarp across the makeshift structure he was able to cloak the body without actually touching it. He just waved at the driver and the little kiddies as the bus went by.

All the children blissfully unaware a woman had come to an agonizing end along their bus route.

Once the Sheriff arrived he called in every available Deputy to do a grid search for any clues while the M.E. went about his ghoulish work.

"Hey, Sheriff, I just found this about a quarter of a mile back!" Deputy Johnson called.

Johnson was wearing latex gloves and held the crucifix up. It glinted dully in the sun inside its clear, plastic, evidence bag.

"Well, our list of possible local victims just got a lot shorter. Larson! Over to the Sacred Heart Church to talk to the priest!"

Just as Larson was about to take the crucifix and go see the padre the medical examiner called "No need. She has i.d. In her pocket. This is little Ciara, Jared Holder's wife."

Larson and Johnson pulled up very quietly, almost reverently, to the Holder place. Motion in the big barn caught Larson's eye. "Hey," he said to Johnson then jutted his chin in the direction of the barn.

Death notifications are the worse and Ciara was such a pretty little thing, shy but sweet.

"Deputies Larson and Johnson here Jared, can we come in?" announced Larson.

"Gentlemen! Greetings, to what do I owe this pleasure?" Jared called out.

Larson noticed a Jack Daniels bottle with just a few pulls out of it on a nearby sawhorse.

Jerad's eyes looked heavy and blurry. Then Larson saw the blood.

"Jerad, now why don't you come out here with us and take a seat?" Once all three men were seated around the firepit where Jerad's murderous plot began Larson continued "Jerad, where did all the blood come from?"

This time Jared knew just what to say "Oh, those damn dogs got in a fight. I had to separate them, it's not my blood." he said grinning, again.

"Well, the reason we're here is because we have some difficult news. When did Ciara last leave the house?" asked Johnson.

Jared looked into the bright sky like he had to think a long time about it. Like the last time he'd seen her leave the house was not after he tied his wife to the back of his truck. "Oh, something at church last night. She must have bible study or something this morning. She was gone before I got up. Didn't even bother to make me breakfast! Women! Huh?"

"Uh-huh" said Johnson who noticed Larson's attention was trained somewhere inside the barn. Then he spoke, "Jared, looks like you had a little accident there." Johnson looked to see what Larson spotted and saw a fairly big dent, it looked like there was blood and hair in it.

The three men got up and approached the truck as Jerad explained "Oh, yeah, I was trying to back up out of a steep ditch out there on the property line. Stupid deer jumped the fence right as I got up some speed, slapped it silly, see… you can see some of its hair right here."

Stroke of brilliance, Jared thought. That dumbass Carl gave him the idea with the information about a deer on the side of the road but the rest was all Jerad including removing Ciara's hair from the truck then using fur off one of the deer carcass hanging in the barn and rubbing it off into the dent.

He looked up to see Johnson and Larson exchanging a look between themselves then into the open back door of the truck. The duffel bag sat there open with ropes, some zip ties, his new taser, and the bloody knife.

The panic in Jared's eyes was sufficient even if the two experienced deputies didn't already know they were looking at some kind of murder or rape kit.

Jared, I need you to raise your hands and step away from the truck.

"She made me do it! The stupid bitch MADE ME! You didn't know her. She lived to push my buttons and she pushed too far."

It was an ugly display Jared put on at the defense table next to his attorney after the jury's guilty verdict was read aloud.

In an instant deputies cuffed his wrists, shackled his feet, and pushed him back into a seated position. The one in charge, a big black bull of a man, whispered into Jared's ear "Say something else you prick, I want to put a gag in your mouth. Please say something else."

Jared fell silent. He never did well in confrontations with other men.

Then the jury handed down his sentence. Life in prison without the possibility of parole for the first-degree murder of Ciara Holder.

The Judge rapped his gavel once, thanked the jury members for their service, turned to Jared, and in a somber tone said "May God have mercy on your soul. Though I don't think you deserve it."

All Jared could do was shake his head and cry as he was dragged away.

#trueSTORY
#mixedORIENTATION
#cohabCOUPLES

It takes a Village, People

My lovemaking with Debbie on that steamy Houston afternoon in 1979 was, as always, very good. Actually, it was pretty mind-blowingly-great.

I suppose the fact my brain was still vibrating from my orgasm and the contact high of Debbie's multiple orgasms is why I did not speak the truth to my lover. Had I spoke the truth it would have been "Debbie, I'm gay."

No, instead I went with "Debbie, we should get married."

In retrospect that wasn't very smart.

I led Debbie with blinders on into a mixed-orientation marriage. That's what it's called when you enter into the institution of marriage appearing to be a heterosexual couple when one of you is actually gay. And in our case, only one of us knew it.

Some gay guys get married thinking they're straight. Others do it wishing they were straight. Those imagine somehow marriage will fix them. Not that marriage fixes anyone or anything in reality.

Mixed orientation marriages are still pretty common today and definitely, gay guys were doing it in droves in the '50s, '60s, and '70s. An entire segment of gay guys became homophobes. Hating what they were so much they'd even turn to marriage for a solution.

In a mixed-orientation marriage it often comes down to the same hitch as in marriages between two heterosexual people, if the wife would just allow infidelity the marriage would work like a charm. Most women are not up for an open relationship especially when only the guy is partaking outside the partnership.

I'm still not sure, all these years later, why I didn't tell Debbie the truth. I'd broken it off with past girlfriends by revealing I love men and having sex with them. I also love a great romp with a beautiful woman. As any self-respecting bisexual does.

And while we have our very own "B" in the LGBT umbrella label, identifying as bisexual makes you a bit of an outcast among both straights and gays.

You're viewed as either confused, greedy, or just a basic unbridled horn dog. Everyone else is trying to pick from just 50% of the population while bi-folk has all four-point-three billion people on this big, blue, marble to choose from.

That was the world population in 1979, anyway. Gasoline prices were .86cents a gallon and a dozen eggs cost

.85cents.

A Pakistani mob destroyed the U.S. Embassy in Islamabad and HIV/AIDS was about to destroy hundreds of thousands of lives when it went viral. Not the good 21st century meaning of viral "Woo-hoo, my video of me catching popcorn in my belly button just went viral!!!"

AIDS was a never-ending viral crush of waves of infection attacking people at the cellular level and refusing to ever be cured.

A real son of a bitch.

And because humans are basically assholes and need to make anything bad all about others rather than themselves it was dubbed the gay virus. Like COVID was called the Chinese virus. Untrue but, people are assholes.

I guess I was an asshole, too.

I should have told Debbie right off the bat I was bisexual.

But I wanted children and I wanted to be a dad so I didn't tell her.

I knew Debbie didn't have a problem with people being gay, per se.

Cruising and Scoring.

Of course, she'd prefer the as-advertised straight husband she signed on for, but the big picture, she knew my brother was gay, my sister, too. She accepted them for who they were and had no problem with who they loved romantically.

Handy tidbit for straight people, being gay absolutely runs in families so if you're dating someone who has gay siblings or first cousins you need to half expect that your significant other swings wide to the other side of the Kinsey scale from where you are.

I'm one of seven children and four are as vanilla straight

as anyone can be so take from that what you will. There are no guarantees in this life but be aware gays are rarely hanging out as a single, solitary, fruit on the branch of any family tree.

I didn't tell Debbie I knew that.

I should have told her that while she was nursing our firstborn child I was out catting around, cruising and scoring with any cute guy who would have me. And there were a lot of them who had me. Maybe a metric ton of dudes.

I should have told Debbie that while I did love her, the only way for our marriage to last was for her to sign off on me having carnal relations with a lot of other people, specifically men. I didn't tell her so she didn't have a chance to pick a different path, separate from me.

I lived a double life which was the root of our bifurcation, our eventual separation then our divorce.

One guy I dated was the choir director at one of the many, local, Baptist churches. It seemed to me that was just asking for heaping helpings of guilt but we were just tricking so what he did throughout the majority of his life had nothing to do with me.

He supplemented the small Jesus paycheck by waiting tables at Red Lobster. And that's exactly where Debbie's parents wanted to take us for dinner one evening during one of their bi-annual visits to view the grandchildren.

I couldn't think of a single excuse to avoid the restaurant. And being pre-cell phone prevalent times I had no way of giving my trick boy a heads up that the entire straight family was incoming.

He told me later as soon as he saw us at the reception desk he went straight to the kitchen and threw up. Which got him sent home for the night. Affording my family and most especially me a meal free from distractions or messiness.

I treated my marriage like a safety net. My upstanding, respectable, safety net of a straight relationship to fall back on whenever it suited me.

Being a married man proved to be a powerful aphrodisiac to the gays. Absolutely no possibility of a commitment meant fuck buddies were easy to find and easy to leave.

One guy I hooked up with regularly drove a minivan with a rear-facing baby seat in the back. One day I asked about his wife and kid thinking maybe I'd found a kindred soul, someone else in a mixed-orientation marriage.

Not the case.

Brad explained "Oh, I got that at Goodwill, it keeps guys from getting ideas about trying to date me or some shit. They think I'm on the down low, getting some of the nasty on the side while the wife and kid are home. (chuckles) It makes life so much easier."

I suppose I was using the same trick. Except rather than a fictional family without substance or feelings I was using live human beings, but still to the same end as Brad. Keep the hookups easy to find, and easy to leave.

I'd leave fully satisfied and head home to my wife and children and I really should have told Debbie all of it well before our firstborn turned 14.

But that is when I did it. In 1995 when Caleb was 14 and Ethan was five I told Debbie I like men. I like having sex with them and I have been doing so for pretty much the entirety of our marriage.

In my mind, I think I expected she'd celebrate my honesty, my newfound truth, my decision to come out of the closet and be me.

I didn't expect she'd throw me a Pride parade but I thought

the slap across my face was a little over the top.

I'd done the right thing! I'd told her the truth and she was all "Gary, if you have AIDS I'll kill you!" "Gary, you've ruined my life!" "Gary, you tore me away from my family!" "Gary, I'll be abandoned!"

Sheesh, this isn't about you Debbie!

I really believed that. Looking back from the vantage point of 25-plus years of hindsight I was really an asshole.

Once I came out to my wife we decided to do what so many people in mixed-orientation marriages do. We tried to make it last, anyway. We had a shared home and two beautiful children, so much to fight for. We went to counseling even as we moved into separate bedrooms.

I didn't stop getting my jollies on the side and one day Debbie flat out said she wanted no more counseling, she wanted a divorce. I think she was trying to shock me into waking up to our reality and the seriousness of the situation. The bifurcating fork in the road where we were standing above a high cliff and I just viewed it as a hall pass.

To me separation seemed like a common enough word for a common enough occurrence. Calling it quits.

Debbie felt all the depth and breadth and nuances of what it means to separate.

Literally to disconnect, split, to sever. We were about the business of taking our marriage and dispersing it through space. Debbie fully felt the definition of separation meaning to block off, isolate, divide, dislocate, detach, withdraw, to be out of relationship with anyone, to exist by oneself.

I viewed it as a common occurrence but, to exist by oneself, is absolutely not common. It is gut-wrenchingly life-changing and soul-damaging. But I didn't get that at the time.

Ever the efficient engineer I took the most direct path. I moved into a rental near our home and I kept paying the mortgage and all the household bills for Debbie and the boys.

Then I decided we needed to spread my truth more widely. We needed to tell the boys the marriage was ending and exactly why.

Debbie was vehemently opposed.

She tried to reason with me that the kids didn't need to be hit with both the divorce plus the added confusing layer of who's gay, straight, or bi much less what any of that means.

But I was the father and I knew best so I sat the kids down, Debbie glaring daggers into the back of my head from the next room the whole time and I told them "Your mom and

I are getting a divorce. It doesn't have anything to do with you guys it's because I'm gay."

Little Ethan ran upstairs to his room in tears. I was confused because at the tender age of five he had no idea what "gay" meant. Now I realize his reaction was likely due to hearing "gay" used as a slur in the schoolyard and whatever it was he certainly didn't want his dad to be it.

My eldest just excused himself and went I don't know where because with that all done and dusted it was time for me to keep on keepin' on.

My boys could have grown up hating gays because of what I'd done. It's easy to lump everyone into the same cart with that one bad apple. They didn't though.

Ethan still tells the story of his best friend coming out to him in college.

The two worked as waiters on the same schedule so every

week they'd go to a matinee and grab lunch together.

His friend was so nervous, afraid he was about to lose his best friend, and when he told Ethan "I'm gay."

Without missing a beat Ethan said "Fuck, man! My DAD'S gay what else have you got?!"

It's still funny and those two are still friends. I have to cling to any positives I can find because at the time I was tearing our marriage apart I was fairly oblivious to anyone's pain.

Joseph.

Because by this time I'd met Joseph.

We were in love and quickly started talking about having a baby of our own.

While Debbie viewed the separation and divorce as the death of her life, I viewed it as my ticket to true love and the doorway to the rest of my life.

That was callous and it was cruel. I'd never set out to hurt the woman I married, I just couldn't see past my own single-minded desires for my life or past the tip of my dick.

I was paying her bills, what more could she possibly want?

She wasn't sure herself what she wanted so she cast a wide net.

She repeatedly threatened to out me at work and end my career. Rather than showing any remorse for the obvious emotional pain I'd caused and continued to cause her I'd come back with something shitty like "Go ahead, where do you think the money will come from, then?!"

I was actually scared shitless about the possibility of being outed. It was perfectly fine to come out on my own terms to only those I wanted to tell but, whoa Nelly, let's just back off of this truth in the workplace stuff.

Cases of HIV and AIDS continued to rise and to kill. The entire gay community, and gay guys, in particular, were being further stigmatized and blamed for spreading the scourge to innocent straight people. Which, if you think about the mechanics of exactly what that entails the math doesn't work. But, scape-goating makes the "normal" people sleep better wrapped in their own self-righteousness at night.

Debbie's next move was to demand copies of all bank statements and expense reports for the past five years. Joseph and I spent many a night after work hours making copy after copy to be boxed up and dropped off at Debbie's attorney's office.

Then I did something I hadn't done with Debbie since the separation. I had a thoughtful, reasonable, conversation. I denied that to Debbie but I sat down with her best friend to talk over the state of our affairs. Olivia and I agreed slogging through this long, drawn-out, divorce was only hurting all involved.

I lamented "Olivia, why can't Debbie see that her demand for a five-year paper trail is only taking money away from the children and feeding it to the attorneys? Plus it's dragging things out for far too long, I need to get on with my life."

I'd always liked Olivia because she's bright, a great friend and she never minced words so I guess I shouldn't have been surprised when she said "You really are just a big ol' self-involved asshole, aren't you?! Wake up Gary this is not about you it's about the abuse you've heaped on Debbie!"

I was indignant "I have never, ever, raised a hand to Debbie or the children!"

"No just both of your figurative middle fingers in a

constant salute for the past 15 years and counting." Olivia shot back. "Can't you see you've lied, you've cheated, you've lied about cheating and all of a sudden you want a mother fucking medal for coming out?! Grow up, you selfish little boy!"

This was not at all the way I envisioned this conversation going. I expected Olivia to get in lockstep with me and push Debbie on through the divorce to freedom.

My dating and married life with Debbie flashed before my eyes and it brought me to my knees in tears of shame and remorse. Then came the shame for how I'd been behaving during the separation and on the road to divorce. None of this was working. None of this was right.

Debbie was beautiful, brilliant, and kind. I claimed her as my own purely because I wanted offspring and needed a breeding receptacle.

I had abused her.

So many times I refused her hugs or even to hold her hand because my mind was on my next lay.

How horribly lonely for her. I'd forced her into an existence void of even the most basic level of intimacy, like an emotional sensory deprivation tank.

No wonder she'd been acting crazy. I'd driven her mad with my news that our entire relationship and our lives together were a fabrication. I added insult to injury by being sarcastic and shitty to her, annoyed it was taking her so long to get over it.

I'd been over it before we took our wedding vows. I never stopped to consider the immense heartbreak and shock I'd caused to Debbie without a backward glance.

I talked to Joseph, I talked a lot with Olivia.

Then finally I talked with Debbie.

Our call began with her usual bitch-fest and list of all

the ways I was failing our children. I took it all without reaction.

Then I said "Debbie, I deserve all that and more. Please hear me, all I want is for you to be happy."

The Apology, The next S-O-B.

At first there was only stunned "Then why in God's name did you MARRY me?!?!?"

And I told her.

I apologized for all the lies. I told her she's a great woman, a fantastic mother, and a better friend to me than I could ever deserve.

Then I told her to find someone else. "I get that you're pissed off at me, rightly so. But, if all you do on your dates is talk about what an S-O-B your ex-husband is, well, no one wants to be the next S-O-B in your story. I hurt you. You deserve real love and I know he's out there for you.

You've earned it."

While Debbie never did remarry or get serious with another guy I found out many years later that conversation did have its desired effect.

I was having dinner with Caleb and Ethan. Caleb was about to get married and Ethan had a serious girlfriend and I wanted to impart my late-in-life wisdom about not being an asshole and helping others when you can, especially those you've wronged.

So I told them the "no one wants to be the next S-O-B in your story" conversation.

Caleb and Ethan just looked at each other, jaws dropped. "So THAT'S what happened!"

I looked between them confused and Caleb explained "It was like a light switch was flipped one day. Mom went from dark back to light. She stopped complaining about you, really she didn't complain about anything she just got up and moved forward. We thought she'd joined a cult or something."

Part of me was a little miffed Debbie had not shared with me the positive impact my words had had. Then I checked myself and accepted the fact Debbie didn't owe me any thanks. She didn't owe me anything and still, a little part of me felt cheated. You don't get over being a selfish asshole all at once I'm still a work in progress.

So I ruined marriage for Debbie and the divorce was hell.

I thought I was finally out of the relationship woods, happy with Joseph and making plans to become parents, together.

Turns out that union was doomed, as well. Even though it was born out of honesty between Joseph and myself, it was destined to fail nonetheless. Isn't that just a giant kick in the ass with a steel-toed boot?

Joseph and I had moved to his dream city, Sarasota, Florida.

I hated it from day one.

Sarasota is on the Gulf Coast… the Redneck Riviera for God's sake. It's where the Ringling Brothers Circus went for winters. There were circus freaks everywhere and the smell of exotic animal dung mixed with the shallow water rot scent that seemed to lightly coat everything.

But it was all for my Joseph, the man I loved, and we bought a house.

We bought our house just as the bottom dropped out of the economy and we were left scrambling for work of any kind. And, no, running off and joining the circus was not an option.

Joseph endured some IT work for a large retailer, hating every moment of it.

I traveled a lot because I'd have to go wherever oil and gas companies needed an engineer even as that entire industry floundered. I visited the boys whenever I could and was never once even a day late with the child support. No one was happy but that's marriage and divorce for you.

I resented Joseph for putting us in that position but at the same time, I loved him deeply. We were committed and faithful and that just had to be worth something.

Of course, by this time we were both gentlemen of a certain age and if I'm completely honest the sex drive was waning. I realized morality is actually controlled by a person's sex drive, not by morality. Don't tell the church folk.

But we plodded along until Joseph was offered his dream job writing code and creating languages for various companies' computer systems across the U.S. It meant a move but at this point even Joseph was ready to see the backside of Sarasota for good.

We moved to the city of brotherly love, got back on firm financial footing, and found a surrogate who would eventually bring us Elliott.

Since I was a dad I didn't feel like I could deny Joseph the same experience. Even though at this point our relationship was on the rocks and a baby is definitely not a relationship bandaid.

We did the whole sperm soup method. A laboratory mix of my spunk and Joseph's but the morning Elliot was born it was crystal clear whose sperm had won the race to the egg.

Rather than feeling Elliot has two dads, Joseph's primal urge to successfully procreate good stock seemed to take over and he immediately felt he was the father and I simply was not.

I have only one photo of all three of my sons together. I had Caleb and Ethan come to Philadelphia to visit one summer. They didn't get along with Joseph, Elliott had screamed squarely into the middle of his terrible twos. Once again, no one was happy.

So I'd go visit my boys, Joseph would stay home with his boy and just as Elliott hit double digits Joseph decided it was over between us and he was going to keep Elliott from me.

We had the custody battle, I was paying child support throughout, and afterward even as Joseph kept me away from the boy who legally was every bit as much my son as my biological kids.

Joseph's primal urges went into overdrive and he got ugly. When Elliot was eleven years old Joseph told him he, dad Joseph, wouldn't leave Elliot alone with me because I'd snatch him up and take him away forever. Joseph invited me to exit their lives forever and I guess I was just too tired to fight anymore. I did as Joseph asked and I haven't seen Elliott in ten years.

Once in a while I search him up on LinkedIn, it looks like he's become a pretty successful chef.

To Debbie's credit, she's never laughed in my face following my separation. The split from Joseph and Elliott. My relationship detachment, leaving me to exist all by myself. Now severed from my second marriage and my third child.

She deserves a medal for keeping a civil tongue in her head on the subject because I was, in many ways, living through the same type of heartbreak and shock I caused Debbie.

One marriage was entered like I was a drag queen dressing up and playing a straight guy. And that didn't work.

The next marriage was entered into by two people who were living honest lives, open about our sexual orientations and our relationship.

That didn't work either.

I do have a good relationship with both Caleb and Ethan. They make me proud every day.

I risked ruining that for all of us because I didn't tell Debbie the truth that steamy Houston afternoon so many years ago. I lied and I cheated and in the end, I still get to have my two sons. I got lucky. That's all there is to that. I didn't earn it, I just got lucky. At least now I appreciate being their dad and their friend.

I make a ton of money. I hook up whenever I feel like it. Which isn't often these days but it's nice to know I have options. I refuse to believe the number of options I have is in direct correlation to the number of dollars I have.

I'm paying the bills so I can write whatever version of my life, and the lives of those I intersect with, as I please. That's what I've always done. It generally hasn't worked but I see no reason to change things up now.

#trueSTORY
#gay
#straight
#sinners
#saints

George Adam Yellow

The explosion shook our house and blew Tom across the room.

We were newlyweds coming up on our first wedding anniversary and I was trying to make some dinner rolls from scratch. The oven wouldn't heat up. Tom joined in the ef- fort. "Sandra, the pilot light is out! Leave it to a woman to miss the fact there's no fire to light the fire!"

Well he sure showed this little lady!

What neither of us took into consideration was the 15 minutes we spent tinkering and fiddling with the stove, gas was running and filling our tiny kitchen.

So, the moment Tom sparked the pilot light to life it caused an explosion. Tom ended up with a concussion, and it burned off his eyebrows, beard and all of his arm hair. I never cared for that beard. Bit of foreshadowing, that.

The only reason I wasn't beside him as the natural gas ignited in a fiery ball was be- cause I was pregnant with our first child and I really had to pee.

I rushed him to the hospital and my cowboy was patched up good as new… though mostly hairless.

On the way home I got to giggling and could not stop. For a second Tom's male ego was bruised because his woman was laughing at him. I couldn't help myself. All of the

fear and stress melted away in grateful, relieved, laughter and tears over the absurdity of the entire situation. Plus my pregnancy hormones were raging.

Soon Tom was laughing right along with me. I had to pull over. I could barely breathe or see through my hysterical tears. We were both laughing and hugging and rocking each other.

If you take out of the equation being bound for eternity in the eyes of God to my hus- band who I did not love, and the cringe-worthy sex, we had an excellent marriage. We were best friends. We enjoyed each other's company very much.

I'd never had sex before my union with Tom. My first kiss was with Tom. We were both raised in a small, rural town where everyone practiced big religion. Heavy on the judgement and damnation and light on the whole "Do unto others as you would have others do unto you" and "Love thy neighbor as thyself"

If Tom followed the Golden Rule surely he would not have raped me?

I tried to explain to him over and over it just felt wrong. I asked him to imagine if soci- ety said he should only have sex with other men, how would he feel? That pissed him off every time. Tom wasn't having it and he'd have sex with me, anyway. I'd hold a pil- low over my head and cry as Tom would rape me and yell "That's right, you should be ashamed, you should cover your head!"

Of course 1980 in the deep south there was no such thing as raping your wife. Hell, it's the same story in 2021 for many women.

Over the years, from the outside we looked like the picture of marital bliss and success. We were comfortable financially.

Our two beautiful boys were my entire reason for being. Both being the product of rape did not seem to touch either their temperaments or personalities. Hard working, gentle and kind souls, both of them.

Henry arrived just after our first wedding anniversary. Sweet little James joined seven years later.

I was a police officer. Tom built homes and tended cattle.

On the job I responded to sexual assault calls but never once considered making a re- port about the crimes going on in my own home.

Even if I'd made a report, even though I was quickly rising to the rank of detective on the force, it wouldn't have gone anywhere. Can't have women thinking they have a say in their husband's home, his castle.

Plus, most locals already thought I was far too big for my britches, what with the fact I went to college and earned my criminal justice degree before joining the local police de- partment.

It's always been so odd to me, I wanted to protect and serve everyone in my community. Even though many of them wouldn't have crossed the street to spit on me if I was on fire.

No one could exactly put a finger on what made me so distasteful. But I had a good husband and good boys so I was deemed worthy of being part of polite society.

Reflecting on it all, "To thine own self be true" was uttered regularly. Usually with an ac- companying wise nod. But what it actually meant in our town was; be your true self as long as you're just like your neighbors on all four corners of your country lane.

That's what started the ball rolling when Tom and I met at a 4th of July party. He was 24 and I was 20. He was a handsome cowboy, me the pretty little filly who'd caught his eye. This is what it's supposed to look like. Like everybody else.

The engagement story was one befitting a plain-spoken cowboy taking the next logical step in life.

We were in his pickup truck and Tom said "You know, sometimes I think I'd like to get married."

I said "Have anyone particular in mind?"

We both laughed but there was never really a question of who... it was me. Full stop.

If I'd stayed in the marriage I'm certain I would have committed suicide somewhere around 1994.

What Tom didn't know and I didn't know, what a police liuetenant on the force was about to revel to me is, I'm gay. More precicesly I'm a lesbian.

I was so sheltered growing up I never knew my strong desire to be very best friends with one girl or another through my school years were really full-on teenage crushes. I had no idea. One of the girls, Barbara Jean Miller, took to calling me Kiki and the nick- name stuck. Did she know?!? How would Barbara Jean know "Kiki" was a 1940's slang term for lesbian?

Still, it fit.

Noone can tell me being gay, lesbian or bi-sexual is a choice. You simply are or you are not. I didn't know what a lesbian was, how could I possibly have chosen to be one?

I didn't know why I, a straight A student floundered hopelessly through Miss Marshall's english literature class. Looking back I realize I was so mesmerized by the curve of her neck and what her hips did in her skirt I was literally dumbfounded.

I got a C and moved on down the line.

I don't know if my ignorance was a blessing or a curse.

If I were in high school in this day and age I know I would only date girls. A gold-star lesbian from the start.

Coming out would have been impossible in my home,

school or church.

So while I knew something felt wrong about dating, marrying and mating with Tom there simply wasn't another option to my knowledge.

At least I didn't suffer from being forced to stay in the closet. I was just in there trying on straight girl clothes and thought "Well, this is life."

And then there was Brenda. Brenda and I worked the same shift at the police depart- ment. She was a lieutenant, I was a detective by that time around 1990.

I knew she was going through a divorce from her husband. My marriage was also sig- nal-30 by that time. Dead.

That's what we were talking about one night as we sat in my patrol vehicle after our shift.

Brenda was holding my hand as we talked and laughed. Then she was caressing that back of my hand with hers, then she ran her fingers up and down my arm. I leaned in, she leaned in and we kissed. We kissed a lot. I had decades of missed kisses to make up for!

My first reaction the next day was to tell Brenda "Never again. This can never, ever, happen between us again."

My second reaction, about eight hours later, was to sleep with Brenda in her former marital bed.

We were in love. Sparks-flying, birds singing, sun shining on us in love.

But we couldn't be out about it. I was still married, she recently divorced. And the fact "ho-mo-SEX-uality" is not a mental illness, as medical professionals generally catego- rized it until 1973, was not an accepted fact in our town because, God.

Still, I rejoiced silently. I was walking on air, a giddy smile permanently plastered across my face. A mirror image of

Brenda's blissful face but we knew our careers and even our lives were at stake.

We both have friends on other police departments who came out either by choice or were forcibly outed after getting caught with their hand on the kitty. Or mouth on the muff. After that, their urgent Signal 23 -- officer down or needs help -- calls for backup went unanswered.

A fellow officer, the one standing next to you on that thin blue line, would not answer your call for help because of who you love.

That's fucked up. And it's terrifying.

And it wasn't nearly enough to keep Brenda and I apart.

Tom and I had already been talking divorce well before before my lesbian revelation.

We'd moved into separate bedrooms right around the time James was two years old.

Our families did not take the divorce news well. There were many "Christians" praying over our union. Someone may have handled a snake at one point. They didn't know it but they were actually trying to pray the gay away.

I didn't come out to my parents or my brother and sister. I guess I've never officially come out to anyone. One day I was mildly sad all the time and the next I was gay and living my best life,.

I was a better mom, a better friend and a better police officer. Because I was finally whole.

Then came a crushing blow.

My divorce attorney informed me "Tom tells his attorney you're having an affair. He thinks you're some kind of lesbian or something."

I told him I was definitely not "or something."

The attorney turned five shades of red and spat at me

"There's not a judge in this coun- ty that will give you custody of your kids if you're ho-mo-SEX-ual!"

I felt panic like I'd never felt before in my life. Active shooter situations and rape at the hands of the man I married were nothing compared to my mama bear reaction to the possibility of losing my boys.

Thankfully, Tom became an ally. He didn't know what an ally in the LGBTQ+ community

was and neither did I but he stood up for me. Placing my value as a mother above my sexual orientation.

Tom's even cowboy wisdom took over where his hurt feelings had been. I mean, turn- ing your wife gay is a blow to any man's ego. It doesn't work that way, of course, but I know it's how Tom viewed the situation.

In the end he approached our lives going forward as a practical matter.

He quickly recognized our boys' lives and even his life would be better with me in the middle of it all. I believe that was our true God at work there. The Golden Rule in ac- tion.

Being a pragmatic man anxious to have plenty of sex with bona fide women who like penis he shut down that homophobic unwritten rule that gays can't parent.

Tom went to his attorney and told him I'm an amazing mom. He told that attorney we'd share custody and he better never tell a judge or anyone else about my affliction. That's how Tom became an awkward ally for gay rights. All that mattered were the results.

We co-parented our boys and stayed friends.

Brenda and I moved in together. By that time our relationship was the worst kept secret in the county. You can resist taking your love's hand in public. You can control yourself just enough to keep your palm from caressing her beautiful cheek while others are watching.

You can control your words and actions but not your face.

The look shared between two people in love can't be hidden.

Fortunately by the mid-90's there had been some progress both in rights for queer folk as well as more acceptance of those who are "other" in the workplace. Brenda and I were able to live happily as a couple, as long as we were very quiet and discreet about it.

We were grown women with children and a home and our careers. But we were acting like a couple of lovestruck teenagers.

One night after work we got into the swimming pool at the local high school and went skinny dipping. We made love and we laughed.

If we'd been caught we'd have both been booted off the

force, without our pensions, in a hot minute.

I'd lived 35 years on this planet and I'd never been in love before. If you've never been in love you just assume you have been. I thought I'd loved Tom. I had friendship love for him but I'd never had romantic love before Brenda.

One night, Brenda planned to go to a concert with her parents. I declined Brenda's invi- tation to join.

Then something unnerving happened, but for

The South in America at the time, wouldn't strike anyone with surprise.

Her parents barely tolerated me as Brenda's roommate and made a point of preaching about the sins of ho-mo-SEX-uality and being a sodomite in God's eyes whenever I was around. Heavy emphasis on how all such sexual deviants would burn forever in hell fire. "Turn or Burn" they said.

Ok Steve and Karen, y'all have fun with that.

It was after midnight and no sign of Brenda after the concert. They were going to see Steven Curtis Chapman. It was unlikely it had turned into a drunken rave.

I dozed off, I woke up around 1 a.m. with Brenda knocking on our bedroom window. She didn't have her keys, she was shaking and crying.

I wrapped her in blankets and held her tight as she told me her parents had pulled the old Christian music concert bait and switch.

They'd taken her to a larger city about two hours away from our home where they'd hired an exorcist. Yes, really.

No one's catholic but they found someone who claimed he could cast out those carpet munching demons for good. For five thousand dollars. So much for Christian charity.

Brenda literally escaped with only the clothes on her

back and hitchhiked home. Her parents were clearly more concerned about which way Brenda swings over any thought about her life and her safety.

As the sun came up we were both over the shock and, as we would do many times over the years we ended up laughing about it.

I could just imagine the exorcist having a pen full of pigs he'd pretend to drive demons into then chase them into the lake to drown. That's how it was done in the Bible I fig- ured Steve and Karen would want the full monty for their $5-K.

It's amazing the shit people will pull while completely ignoring the Golden Rule.

Why, in the face of true love, do so many people cling to hate and judgement until their knuckles have gone white with the effort?

I'll never understand.

Rather than trying to figure out homophobic straight people... breeders... I launched into learning about being a lesbian. Brenda and I would laugh until we cried watching the Alexis&Lillian YouTube channel.

The one about queer slang had us rolling.

Apparently you can't be just a lesbian.

You're a lipstick lesbian, femme or high-femme depending on your level of girly fashion and makeup aesthetic.

On the other end of the scale are the dykes, butch lesbians with very short hair, no

makeup, ever, who never met a flannel shirt with the sleeves cut off they didn't like.

In the middle there's a chapstick lesbian. Not femme enough to be a lipstick lesbo but not full on butch, either.

Brenda and I both hail from this camp.

A gold star lesbian is one who has never had sex with a man. A lone star lesbian had sex with a man once and immediately decided she only wants innies, no outies when it comes to netherregions.

And you have your "Hundred Footer".

A woman so clearly and fully lesbian you can spot her as such at 100 feet.

Lawd it's funny when the words are used amongst ourselves rather than as weapons by others. Freeing, really.

When we'd go to the nearest lesbian bar, an hour away from home, we'd play a game of trying to identify the different types of lesbians using our queer slang learned from Alex- is&Lillian. Then strike up conversations to see how the lesbian in question self-identi- fied. We had some great conversations and made friends we still have today. Our queer clique.

I'm close with my boys and their beautiful children. James and Henry accept me as I am and they love Brenda, too. James and Henry ended up as Breeders for some reason.

I'm close with my mom and my brother and sister. We operate strictly on a don't ask, don't tell model. I suppose it means I am not 100% authentic but it works for all involved. We're not hurting anyone.

Tom is remarried and happy. He found a woman that actually likes penis. A few years ago Brenda and I got married!

Tom doesn't mean to be an ass but he still refers to our union as 'gay married". I sup- pose some tigers really are just big pussies who can't change their stripes.

The other day on the way to Henry's house we got a flat

tire. We're fully capable of changing a tire but we'd fallen into fits of laughter over the old joke: How many lesbians does it take to change a tire?

Ten. One to do it and nine to talk about how gratifying it is without a man.

And just then Tom pulled up, his home is just across a large pasture from Henry's.

He didn't even bother to ask what was so funny. One look at us I'm sure he really didn't want to know.

In his cowboy way he simply changed the tire, tipped his hat to us both and we all drove off into the sunset.

#trueSTORY

Fill my Purpose

I'm riding my bike as fast and as far as I can. Because maybe if I can't breathe and my legs are killing me my brain will stop making me think about how now I've killed two marriages.

People are always saying there's a reason for everything, everything has a purpose but I don't think they mean me. I have no idea what my purpose is because it seems like only bad things happen around me. At 16 years old shouldn't I have SOME idea of my purpose in life?

Maybe my purpose is to keep mom from having a husband.

Because I'm two for two right now. It's sad for her because the most important thing in her life is being married. It's what she wants more than anything. She would have given me up for adoption to stay married to my dad. But he left so fast after I was born she never had a chance to make the offer.

That was the story I was told more often than any bedtime fairy tale growing up, I will never ever EVER get married. It's so stupid. I think marriage makes perfectly normal people stupid.

God, why can't I exercise these thoughts away? Maybe what I need instead of exercise is an exorcist. Haha! At this point I'm willing to try anything to get rid of the million questions and doubts and thoughts that will not leave me in peace.

I have to pull over and rest. Sweat is pouring into my eyes so they sting like fire and I can barely see. I think seeing is very important as you're barreling down any road at top speed. If you don't see what's coming you'll get hurt.

What happened with dad, with mom's second husband, no one saw coming and a lot of us got hurt.

Lester is my dad because he married my mom when I was less than a year old. So he's the only dad I've ever known.

So, I didn't know it was really weird that he insisted I still sit on his lap to watch t.v. when I was 12, 13, 14 years old. I didn't know he should not have put his hands on my crotch as we sat there. I didn't know what was pushing up against my lower back from behind.

By the time I started figuring it all out it was too late and my dad took my virginity when I was 14 years old. He told me it was my purpose. He is a youth pastor at our church so I guess I assumed he'd know my purpose. Plus I love him and I know he loves me, why else would a man take on someone else's daughter to raise? There's a really evil answer to that question that I couldn't grasp until recently.

Every time before it started he'd quote Ephesians 2:10

That's where the apostle Paul says, "We are God's handiwork, created in Christ Jesus to do good works, which God prepared in advance for us to do." Lester said I was tailor-made just for him.

How the hell was I supposed to give that disgusting shit a name when I'd never so much as slow danced with a boy, before?

Getting back on my bike to go visit Vickie I tried to pinpoint exactly when I realized what dad was doing was not ok. I know when I found out it was criminal. That was after my school counselor asked me very direct questions after our foreign exchange student told on dad for doing the same things to her.

Bhavna is her name. She's from India and she's one year older than me to the exact day.

Last year we had a "Birthday Twins" party and it was amazing! Everything was purple, Bhavna and my favorite color. There were balloons and games. We had a huge birthday cake and we all got to drink as much pop as we wanted! We also got to invite any girls we wanted to so there were about thirty people there. It was epic.

Usually I didn't get a birthday party so Bhavna is the bringer of wonderful things in my opinion.

As it turns out we have even more in common than a May birthday and loving the color purple.

Dad had also been raping her for the past year.

She was so terrified she'd be sent back to India in disgrace, ending her education, she kept her mouth shut. Until something made her butt bleed. I don't know what happened but I do know that's when she decided she needed help to make it stop.

I don't know more details because the police told us all not to talk to each other about what happened. Because it could "taint" the criminal case. Things were already beyond tainted but we did as the police asked.

Tiffany, Jodie, Judith, my best friend Vickie, Bhavna and me. The police said we'd all give our information separately to a nice lady at a special place called an advocacy center. And they'd video tape it and that way any of the officials assigned to the case can watch it and we don't have to tell over and over.

The detective on our case told me "You'll tell Miss Kelly all that happened. She'll ask you questions and the only rule is that you tell the truth. That's it!"

"And I'll never have to talk about it again after that?" I asked, feeling relief rush over me. "I can tell someone, once."

"Good girl, that will be it!" encouraged the detective.

Well that was a big, fat, lie. I had to testify against him

once in court a few months ago at something called a hearing and I have to do it again tomorrow at his trial.

We all do. Tiffany, Jodie, Judith, Vickie, Bhavna and me. All members of the worst club ever and one we definitely didn't ask to be in. Dad recruited us all.

The attorney trying to send Dad to prison is named Brian. He's a nice man and he's really, REALLY, mad at Lester. Even more mad than mom is I think. But maybe she's just mad she's not going to be married anymore, again, and it's because of me.

Brian tells me "The police officer didn't exactly lie to you Crystal. With so much evidence he probably thought your dad would want to take a plea… a sentencing offer… rather than drag you all up on the stand but that's not what your dad, it's not what Lester, decided to do."

He pronounced "Lester" like he had something rotten and slimy in his mouth.

I cried "Then why can't I decide I don't want to?! Can't the judge just watch the videos and decide?"

"Unfortunately, no. And it's really unfair." I thought Brian might start crying "Defendants have more rights than victims, it's just the way the system is set up to make sure no innocent people end up in prison. I believe you. All of you. I'm going to do my best to put Lester in prison for a very long time. I need you to stick with me, ok?"

I just nodded. What else could I do?

I pull up to Vickie's house and she's sitting on the front porch crying. Her mom is holding her and they're just kind of rocking back and forth. Looks like it would feel really nice.

Vickie sees me and comes flying off the porch to hug me. Vickie's a hugger. I am not much of a hugger. Generally I don't like anyone touching me in any way. But I accept hugs from Vickie because it seems so important to her.

Plus I'm the reason she's a member of the Tween & Teen Sexual Assault Club. If we weren't friends it never would have happened to her. Probably.

All in a rush she says "I'm scared out of my mind Crystal! I don't think I can go into court again tomorrow with him there. What if no one believes us? What happens if he just walks away and he's mad at us for telling, what do you think he'll do?!?"

I told Vickie what a few people, mainly teachers at school, were telling me "You are brave, you are strong, you can do this."

It's bullshit when people say it to me and it is bullshit me saying it to Vickie but I didn't have anything else. Except the page of my journal that was filled with questions exactly like those Vickie just asked me.

It reads:

Why do people like dad do sex things to girls?

Why don't people believe what's happening right under their noses?

What do we do if all the girls have to do this all over again on another day?

What if the jury doesn't believe us?

What if all of this is for nothing?

What do we do if he walks and he wants to do something to us for telling?

When will these questions go away?

Should I take counseling?

Am I going crazy?

"Crystal, where'd you go?" Vickie asked, shaking my shoulders gently.

"Oh, nowhere. I think I'm just tired from my bike ride" I assure her and offer just enough of a smile to move things along.

Her mom brings out lemonade and those really fancy cookies with really fancy names like "Pirouette" and "Milano" and there's a big stack of the kind with raspberry jam in the middle because she knows those are my favorite.

"Thanks Mrs. Martin! This is awesome!" I say.

I thought I saw just a shimmer of tears along the bottom lids of her eyes then Vickie swept into her mom with a big hug and a "Thank you mom! I love you!"

"Sweetheart I love you so much and I'm so proud of you. You, too, Crystal."

Thankfully Mrs. Martin, like the police, didn't want us

talking about what Lester did.

I turn to Vickie "Damnit. Lester. He's just Lester the molester. I am never calling him dad EVER again." Then before I could stop I just blurted out "Vickie I'm so sorry I didn't want it to happen to you or to anyone and I'm sorry!" and I just started bawling.

Vickie pulls me up the porch steps and we sit in the big swing. She's holding me like her mom was holding her when I pulled up and I was right, it DOES feel nice.

That and some fancy cookies and I'm feeling all better. As good as it gets, anyway.

"I have to go, mom says I need new shoes for the trial so I don't look like trash in front of all those strangers." I explain to Vickie.

"Crystal I hate how your mom talks to you. I can't believe Cheryl is such a bitch. You don't deserve that, you're a good person."

I am good. Other than being a marriage killer but I don't voice that thought to Vickie.

I take it slow on the way home because I really don't want to go there.

I start daydreaming about Mrs. Martin being my mom. Or at least that my mom would have kicked Lester out when she saw what was going on. She could have divorced him. That would have been so much better. Except the part where she wouldn't be married. I know for sure mom knew because I know she reads my journal.

I think the only reason she finally decided to believe me is because Bhavna forced her hand by trying to avoid being raped anymore. I think mom was jealous of Bhavna because of how much, and how often, Lester paid attention to her.

He was still giving me attention, too. And other girls.

It didn't occur to me until recently, but Lester was always the one who arranged every sleepover.

I would never have asked a friend to come over knowing what went on in our house in the dark. But Lester was the youth pastor and parents didn't ask questions and didn't think twice about sending their daughters for the night.

Right into the lion's den.

Since we can't talk about it, I don't know what happened, exactly, to Bhavna, Tiffany, Jodie, Judith, and Vickie. I do know Lester is charged with sex crimes against all of us.

I read that the majority of rape victims never report to police. And kid rape victims usually don't report until they become adults, if at all. It makes my head spin to think Lester likely did this not only to the six of us but probably 18-20 girls.

Dear Jesus.

I do know Lester had a rule that guests sleep on the couch, not in my room with me "So everyone can get a good night's sleep."

There were to be no sweet dreams where Lester is concerned, though.

I've imagined talking with each of the girls. I think it has to be the way I felt when it started. When I look back in my diary, it reads...

I'm so confused. Dad still makes me sit on his lap even though I am twelve! And he puts his hands where my underwear covers and sometimes I think he's moving his fingers on purpose.

On purpose.

But that doesn't make sense because he tells me about purpose and it has to do with God and Jesus "We are God's handiwork, created in Christ Jesus to do good works, which God prepared in advance for us to do." And that I was made just for him.

Maybe I'M using the word PURPOSE wrong. Mom always says I have a lot to learn. I guess this is one of those things.

Just as I reach my house I see mom's car but it's parked all weird, kinda halfway onto the lawn and halfway on the driveway.

I put away my bike and go in the backdoor.

"Mom? I'm home! Why's the car there?" I call.

No answer.

I go on through to the den where the t.v. is playing a rerun of some crime show. Mom is there. She's asleep.

I'd like to just let her sleep and avoid the shoe shopping but I know she'll be really pissed if she has to take me to court looking like trash tomorrow.

"Mom? Mom, wake up." I say as I shake her arm.

She drops a big bottle but she doesn't wake up. Whatever it is in the bottle and in the glass on the side table smells nasty! And it made mom really tired.

I decide to check back on her after I get a drink of water. And maybe bring her one, too.

I go to the kitchen and notice the laptop is open and turned on. Normally it stays in the office, powered down, but there it is on the counter and the cabinet below it is open. This is where Lester keeps his "dad drinks". He'd always tell me to stay out, never open the cabinet or let any of my friends get in there then he'd quote "Proverbs 20:1 – "Wine is a mocker, strong drink is a brawler, and whoever is led astray by it is not wise."

Then he'd drink.

So mom wasn't asleep, she was blind drunk like Lester liked to get. I don't think I've ever seen mom drunk. I wish she'd wake up so I could see what she's like.

Then I see the email.

From the pastor of our church sent to everyone in the congregation with the subject line: Pray mightily for Lester

Did he keep mom and Lester's email address in the "To:" field on purpose? Or he's just that stupid?

I read out loud mocking Pastor William's over pronunciation of EHHVVV-ERRRRR-YYYYY word-D!

"My fellow followers of Jesus,

As you know our Lester is going through a terribly trying time just as our persecuted savior did.

He is fighting false accusations by his wife and daughter. Other girls, too, it's a crying shame.

Remember the words of God from the good book.

Romans 8:17-18

17 Now if we are children, then we are heirs—heirs of God and co-heirs with Christ, if indeed we share in his sufferings in order that we may also share in his glory. 18 I consider that our present sufferings are not worth comparing with the glory that will be revealed in us.

Lester has huge attorney bills and no money. He's not allowed to see any of his children. So, any money you send to the church we could use to help Lester through this.

Yours in Christ,

Pastor William

"Shit." I say to myself.

I imagine any funds received by the church that "could" go toward Lester's mounting legal fees would not go to Lester at all. But rather re-routed to Pastor William's chosen charity. If I had to guess it would be his boat.

Beyond his own brand of fundraising the pastor's email only served as a rallying point for anger and disbelief aimed straight at us by all of our "brothers and sisters in Christ"

Shit.

I notice the email was replied to.

Oh shit, oh no, oh shit!

Yep.

Mom replied. With "reply all". Of course! Because why WOULDN'T she the day before we all have to go on the stand and be face-to-face with Lester, again.

I read her reply out loud in mom's best passive aggressive, sarcastic, voice. She's not waking up any time soon to hear me doing it.

"William, get real you stupid bible thumper. You know any money you can take in, you'll redirect for the care of your precious boat."

Ha! I #NailedIt on that one.

I keep reading.

"Stepping into a boat doesn't make you Jesus, William. Also, while you're asking all of these things for Lester consider this...

HE FUCKING DID IT!!!!!

He did it all. If you want to quote the bible in this situation how about "Learn to do good; seek justice, correct oppression."

The Lord hath spoken bitches!

Think about praying for Lester's family because he caused all of this but I'm the one suffering!"

And, there it is.

Oh, Cheryl. You're nothing if not consistent. Consistently playing the victim. It doesn't even bother me anymore.

Now she's in there snoring like a 300 pound bear. I guess I better go next door and see if Judith will loan me some shoes for court tomorrow. We've worn the same shoe size since first grade. We think that's so cool because no matter which one of us shoots up an inch overnight, we always share the same shoe size.

It's a ding-dang medical miracle.

When I get home with what I hope mom will view as acceptable trial shoes I make a PB&J and go to my room to confer with my journal.

Flipping through the pages I am reminded how many people had to have known through the years what Lester was doing. But, they turned a blind eye because... I don't know why. Because he's a pastor? Or because it's easier to blame a victim than to offer her help?

I open a new page and write...

Why do we have to go testify tomorrow in front of strangers, just feet from Lester, about the scariest, most painful and absolutely worst things that have ever happened in our lives? We're not the ones who did anything wrong!

Lester gets to sit there and hear us describe all the things he did to us. It's like some sort of play made up of all of his sickness and sins that he gets to enjoy reliving, right from the lips of his victims. And I know he'll enjoy it, why else would he put us all through it, again?

Brian said Lester doesn't even have to take the stand unless he wants to! How is that fair?

I know the courtroom will be filled with church members. There praying for Lester and saying awful things about us members of the Tween & Teen Sexual Assault Club.

Hypocrites, all of them!

The problem with our church is all the people claiming to be Christians. As if saying "I'm a Christian!" gives them a pass to do all the things Jesus WOULDN'T do without a second thought.

It makes my stomach roll over and my head hurts just thinking about it. I'm going to take a shower and go to bed.

----- new journale page, new day

WE DID IT!   LESTER IS GOING TO PRISON FOR SIXTY YEARS!

Ten years for what he did to each named victim I guess? With my 10 year portion of his 60 year sentence do I also get my virginity back? Do I get to forget what he did? Will it stop the nightmares?

No. Knowing a bunch of grown-ups from around our area believed us and Lester did not get away with it has to be enough.

I don't know how juries decide that stuff I just know we

all got to be there holding hands in the front row where Brian had us sit to hear "GUILTY" and watch deputies handcuff Lester and lead him away.

Brian says this time it's really over and we don't have to talk about it ever again, although now we are allowed to talk to each other about it.

I think I'm going to invite all of us girls from the case, I just learned we're supposed to refer to ourselves as "survivors" rather than "victims, I'm going to invite all who survived Lester to come meet up at the park every couple of weeks to ride bikes and if we feel like it, talk about what happened and what it's done to us. What we're doing about it. Since it happened to all of us, maybe together we can figure out how to get better.

Maybe sharing together will make us feel less crazy, less alone, less judged. I'm going to try.

Maybe that's my purpose.

#trueSTORY

Roses are Red
Violet be Cra Cra

The nice policeman again slammed Josh's chest into the patrol car and cuffed him. "What's she saying, now?? Come on man, help a brother out what's she saying now?"

"Man," replied the officer while snugging the handcuffs two clicks too far "guys like you make me SICK!"

At which point Josh decided to exercise his right to remain silent. Clearly his almost ex-wife Violet had spun a story believable enough that Josh was being arrested, yet again.

At least the jail has running water. Josh chuckled to himself.

Being carted away from his lean-to, make-shift, house on three acres of mosquito-infested land his granddad had left him. No water, no electricity but by God, Josh owned it outright! Josh let out another humorless chuckle.

Which brought the officer's elbow in quick contact with Josh's ribcage. "You think this is funny you piece of shit?!"

> " No, this is the exact opposite of funny. Please, just kill me know," Josh pleads earnestly "She's taken it all. She's taken it all and she won't rest until I'm dead so... deal me a solid and just shoot me?"

When Josh said, everything, he meant everything down to the last mosquito.

The officer cringed and shook his head "You're not worth

the paperwork asshole. Guys like you who abuse women like your wife …"

Josh let that wash away, he'd heard it all so many times before from men who'd never been married to a woman like Violet but felt it their duty to serve as her knight in shining armor against him. Police, judges, damn attorneys. Josh crawled deep into his mind and just waited for the next blow. After the slow methodical mind rape from Violet, Josh slowly became dumb to it. Retreating to his mind was the only politically correct way of squashing his anger, more like disgust, there was no more anger left in his emotional cache of feelings.

He understood why the officer was so pissed off. Men who abused their wives or children were truly the scum of the earth. In this situation, though, Josh had never raised a hand to Violet or baby Rose.

But Violet was one hell of an actress. On top of having a killer hot body and a very willing mouth whenever it benefited her.

On the 20 minute ride to the police station, Josh leaned his head against the window, softening his focus so the trees went by in one solid sheet of greens and golds while the motion of the police car lulled him into a semi-hypnotized state.

Plus the car was air-conditioned. "Fuck me running backward," thought Josh "air conditioning has to be God's greatest gift to the world."

And the greatest curse was? Violet Thornton. It was no mistake that the word "Thorn" was in her last name. Their poor daughter was going to be known as Rose Thornton, and with any grace she wouldn't turn out like her mother.

Josh met Violet from the land of "the killer bods and cringe-worthy mouths" two years earlier. She'd just retired from the Army and was moving to a high-paying civilian job just down the corridor from Josh. She was in sales and he, in accounting, at a big pharmaceutical company in the Raleigh-Durham area of North Carolina, U.S.A.

From the first handshake and formal introduction, there were sparks. Sparks plus butterflies. Sparkling butterflies in a roaring, rotating lava of lust. Like when a tornado meets a volcano. A lustcano.

Josh and Violet were nearly inseparable.

For their fourth date, Josh took Violet to meet his mother.

"Oh, Mrs. Bennett," gushed Violet "Your roses! This garden. It's an absolute masterpiece!" I did mention earlier that Violet was an actress of sorts, she knew how to play people.

"Mary, please my dear, call me Mary," mom told Violet with a guarded smile.

The rose garden was Mary's pride and joy. Mary's mantra had always been "A rose blooms among thorns." A romantic way of saying "You get what you get, and you don't throw a fit!" Or "You have to take the good with the bad." Little did Mary know this little metaphorical story would play out in her and Josh's life in a very clear and nasty way.

While Josh never acquired the green thumb gift he always kept some beautiful silk roses around his home and patio as a way of honoring his mom. He noticed people would scoff at his fake flowers as they drove by, but Josh didn't care, it meant a lot to him as a strong tie to his mother.

Violet asked Mary about each and every variety "Which one is best for a beginner?" Violet asked, giving me a look like she both never wanted to leave the gardens and couldn't wait to get me home.

Mary was oblivious, she was in her element as reigning rose Queen "Both the teas and the Knock Out roses are great when you're first starting out because you don't have to deadhead them. They're self-cleaning which makes maintenance almost nothing." Interesting thought, said Violet to herself, a "Deadhead Rose"... self-cleaning, no maintenance. Just add water. If she could just find a "Deadhead Rose" of a man.

"Knock Outs, without a doubt," Josh said while caressing Violet's lower back softly.

After leaving Josh's mom he and Violet stopped at a nursery and picked out six Knock Out rose bushes.

Back at Josh's, the couple set the young plants out across the front flower bed where they were most likely to thrive. Josh had a nice spread, not too extravagant, but nice enough that Violet figured it was worth her putting eyes on it.

Somehow on the way to get the shovel to plant the roses, Josh and Violet detoured to the bedroom and had a frenzied, passionate, fuck session.

Later after planting and watering the little rose bushes, getting cleaned up to go out for dinner with another fucktastic interlude in the shower, Josh asked Violet to be his wife.

It was a whirlwind. Violet insisting "Josh I don't need the big, fancy, wedding. Last year I was bivouacked in a damn desert. I want to marry you and get to a beach ASAP!"

So the new Mr. and Mrs. Bennett had a small wedding, the flowers were all roses intertwined with violets, of course.

Josh's mom stood at his side as his "Mom of Honor" and Violet walked herself down the aisle and gave herself away. Marriage in the country was on a decline, and partly due to vengeful scapegrace's such as Violet. Marriage doesn't work anymore and Josh and his Mother were about to find out why.

Maybe that should have rung some bells and sent up about a million red flags in Josh's head but he was in too deep and he simply thought she was independent and self-sufficient and sexy as hell.

The honeymoon was over before the honeymoon was even over.

After a day of drinking on the beach, Violet was blatantly flirting with the bartender. At one point she let any man at the resort who wanted to do body shots off of her bare skin.

Josh wasn't thrilled but he figured she needed to let loose a little post-wedding. After all, he knew whose bed she'd be in that night all tipsy and horny.

Except it didn't work out that way.

Violet sloshed into the honeymoon suite the next morning at dawn stinking of tequila, sweat, and sex. She didn't even bother to apologize. In fact, she was proudly wearing the bartender's bow tie, her disheveled bikini, and nothing else.

"Make me a cup of coffee for the shower, won't you Josh?" she said in the general direction of her new husband then went into the expansive bathroom.

Josh was so shocked he couldn't make heads or tails of anything so he did the last thing he could remember he was supposed to do which was getting Violet coffee. He made it and delivered it to her in the shower. She did not invite him to join her "Leave the pot." was the only thanks he got. What is wrong with women these days, Josh thought to himself.

 How about parasailing??" chirped Violet when she came back to the master suite, jarring Josh from his tangle of anguish and utter confusion.

" Uh, ok?" stammered Josh.

She just looked so damn amazing in her new, tiny, white, bikini Josh just sort of made himself believe he'd had a nightmare. Her ass looked so perfect in that bikini, a beautiful heart shaped ass, with a model's leg gap. They both went on with the honeymoon as though Violet had not cheated on him with at least one man the first night of their vacation celebrating the two becoming one.

Back on the home front life settled back into a comfortable routine. Josh felt sure, again, he'd married the only woman for him and he worshiped her. At least at this point it was a match made in heaven. Josh was a good dude and he deserved a good woman, so he thought.

Meanwhile Violet was fucking every trainer under age of 30 at the gym.

Ignorance may be bliss but when the knowledge bomb drops, and it always does sooner or later, that fucker comes with a mighty sting.

Still, Josh didn't know at the time Violet had become a mega-ho.

One day, about three months into the business of being married, Violet left work early.

Josh was grinding out the quarterlies and ended up getting home late.

When he walked to the front door, through the patio adorned with expensive silk rose arrangements he felt something was, off.

His key in the lock didn't seem to want to work. He jiggled it this way and that. Just as he finally turned the bolt with his key, the door swung open and there was beautiful Violet. In a strappy, pink, nightgown with a matching robe that flowed behind her like a flock of white doves.

Candles were lit and every vase they owned was filled with Violet's prized Knock Out roses.

"Why Mrs. Bennett you look absolutely intoxicating," smiled Josh.

"Thank you, sweet hubby! I made your favorite dinner. Shall we start with something small?" Violet cooed.

"By all means," said Josh as Violet lead him by the hand into the dining room set for a six-course meal.

At Josh's place was a big, pink, envelope.

"Well, open it silly!" smiled Violet as she poured a bottle of his favorite lager into a frosted glass. "It's just a little something."

Josh opened the envelope ever so carefully. There was one, thin, sheet inside. As he pulled it out he whispered

"Wha? Wha? What?" as he looked helplessly up at Violet.

"Wha, wha, what?" Violet's shy-sounding giggle rippled around the crystal decorating the table "It's our baby! Our baby girl!"

Josh stared intently at the little blob and the dark gray background then he swept Violet up in his arms and kissed her over and over and over.

"Ok, baby on board," laughed Violet.

"Oh, shit, I mean shoot. Honey are you ok?!" stammered Josh.

"Of course, you know I'm made of strong stuff! We didn't know it but our little miracle was already there at our wedding with us. Isn't it exciting?!"

Josh was an only child. None of his friends had any children, yet. So this was the first ultrasound he'd ever laid eyes on. He didn't know the blob in question was far too tiny to be anywhere near four months along, much less determine its sex.

He knew only two things, he adored this woman to infinity and back and he'd do the same for their baby girl.

Baby Bennett made three nine months later and they named her Rose.

Josh was in accounting. It should have been obvious the math was all wrong. Although like most geniuses that revel in larger problems, Josh needed a calculator for simple math and most times had to use the fingers on his hands to do basic adding and subtracting. Had Violet gotten pregnant before the wedding that would have meant a baby that November?

But, she delivered a tiny 5.5-pound baby in early January of the following year. The timing was blatantly off.

Josh never thought twice.

He was also oblivious to how his friends, who were mostly co-workers, would shake their heads sadly as they watched it all unfold.

Mother Mary, however, could do the math without the use of any of her fingers.

When Josh and Violet introduced baby Rose to Mary she stumbled back just a step and grimaced a little.

Josh didn't question the black mop of shiny hair Rose sported along with luxurious black eyelashes. Even though he and Violet were both fair and blonde with blue eyes.

It didn't escape Mary's notice that the baby girl, while beautiful, did not resemble her baby Josh at all.

Once everyone was home from the hospital and settled, Mother Mary invited herself over by bringing food.

Before Josh knew it, Mary had locked herself in the

bedroom with Violet.

Josh was cuddling Rose who could sleep through anything while Mother Mary screamed "A rose blooms among thorns you fucking whore! You bitch! How could you do this to Josh you, you, you fucking thorn!"

Josh froze cold into a statue. Never had he ever heard Mary say the "f" word. He didn't think she knew of the "f" word.

A long silence followed. Josh assumed Violet was getting Mary up-to-speed on whatever mistake caused mom's outburst.

Just then the bedroom door slammed open, almost breaking through the door stop on the wall. It was a fierce and audible "BOOM"!

Mary was barreling toward Josh with a clutch of old photos. Josh's baby photos.

Mary explained "Josh, sweetheart, put the baby down." by this time Violet had swept in and sat under a storm cloud holding the still sleeping Rose.

Mary pressed on "Josh, look. Your baby pictures."

He looked at his baby self. He had large eyes and just barely a halo of white-blonde hair, the same striking color as his eyelashes. Not to mention deep piercing blue eyes.

Mary continued "Josh, God or evolution or whatever makes the most sense to you has a way of establishing paternity right at birth. Newborns almost always look exactly like their daddies."

Josh listened, then he turned and looked at Rose. Bewildered.

Suddenly all he could see was an image, in a flash, in his mind was Rose wearing a bowtie. It was the bartender's kid! The light went on in Josh's head, as his soul slowly quivered and shrunk, he felt like the kid that never got picked to play on the playground team. He felt smaller than small, and knew he had been played. The feeling that you feel when you were played by someone so close to your soul, someone that you trusted fervently, was a horrible corner of depression that no-one should ever have to experience. Why God gave us this emotion, Josh couldn't understand, which led to the "Oh Shit" look on his face.

Violet didn't have a lot to say, unusual for her. All she could offer was "Josh she is yours." Is was creepy silent in the room. Almost like that was the only thing Violet could come up with to break the silence. The air was thick and uncomfortable.

The knowledge bomb was dropped. The sting felt like hellfire.

"I'm leaving." Josh barely managed. He realized he needed

to stand up for himself at this point. Violet turned out to be an evil bitch, and Josh was just now owning up to the reality of his mistake of marrying her. It was about to get worse for him however.

"No, darling, bad idea," said Mary "There will be paperwork...."

"Fine," said Violet "bye stupid fuck-boy."

Josh turned, looking at the vile creature that was his wife. Had she always had scales? He hadn't noticed.

Josh hustled Mother Mary out of the apartment, declined her offer to bunk at her place, and drove straight to his best friend Frank's condo.

" I can't believe I didn't see it," stammered Josh.

Frank shook his head, poured them both another

generous round of scotch, pulled out some cigars and laughed "We couldn't believe you didn't, either!"

Josh could only manage "Wait, Wha? Wha?"

"Oh, shit, sorry man," Frank said putting a steady hand on Josh's shaking shoulder.

"We've all suspected she was playing you. No one stays pregnant for 11 months, then has such a tiny baby? She had to have gotten knocked up in April"

The Bennett's honeymoon. April 10-20.

Frank continued seeming not to notice Josh looked like he was about to get sick "Then as soon as the photo of baby Rose went out around the office, it was certain, that kid doesn't look a thing like you."

"It's the bartender's," Josh offered as though it mattered.

"Say what?" asked Frank.

"The bartender, on our honeymoon, she fucked him and that's his kid," and Josh broke down into tears, retreated into the guest room, and didn't show his face again for four days and nights.

Frank meanwhile put the messages from Mother Mary under the guest room door. Day two Frank began helpfully slipping business cards for divorce lawyers under the door, too. Divorce lawyers that supported "Good Dudes and Good Dads" who had to fight against evil bitches like Violet. Never a word from Violet.

On the fifth day, Josh showered, shaved, and was headed to work. As he walked out the door to his automobile. A leggy brunette looking like she was wearing a Halloween costume that would have been titled "Sexy Businessman" approached all smiles and calling Josh's name. She was looking for a rise, but Josh wasn't having it. He was too depressed.

Just as Josh began to look up to meet her smile with his own she slapped a big envelope into his hand and said "You've been served."

That is when Josh's world tilted right over on its axis. Yep, there was that feeling again, like the world had gone pear-shaped and gravity sucked the soul right out of his belly. Frank had watched the scene play out and caught Josh just as he was about to fall.

"Fucking bitch! Come on Josh we're going to your place," said Frank leading a mostly limp Josh away.

At Josh's the front door stood open. The silk roses were still on the patio but Josh and Frank could see all the way through the house. Every stick of furniture was gone. The bitch cleaned him out.

Frank took Josh by the shoulders and maneuvered him into the kitchen where they stood at the breakfast bar and began reviewing the pile of paperwork.

Frank narrated the situation out loud to Josh, like a children's story time from hell. "She's filed for divorce. For alimony and child support." Frank saw the amounts on the standard court worksheet, but didn't want to say anything yet. Josh was going to get fucked by this bitch, a story that plays out time and time again in divorce courts across the nation.

Josh interrupted excitedly "What?!?! Rose isn't even my kid!." Frank pulled a copy of Rose's birth certificate from the pile and pointed "That your name and signature?"

"Yeah, of course, I thought Rose was mine at the time."

"Doesn't matter, courts go by the baby daddy on the birth certificate until you prove otherwise." Josh will be supporting the bartender's kid until he can prove otherwise. Then Frank said, "Look at the bright side, a close buddy of mine didn't find out his kid wasn't his until the kid turned 18. He paid child support and raised that kid for 18 years, only to discover his real daddy. All of that time and money wasn't refundable. He had an investment and an emotional bond at that point. No turning back. No legal recourse. Just fucked. Well, he did get an amazing kid out of the deal...so there's that."

Frank looked back at the paperwork, flipping the page "Oh, DAH-yum, bro!" Frank said then covered his mouth.

"What?! What else could she do?" Josh's eyes searching his friend's face for answers.

Frank laid out another piece of paperwork filed of record with the court "She got an emergency protective order against you. We gotta go, you can't be in here."

"But it's my house! I was here first!" protested Josh.

"And now it's time to leave, if she shows up or calls the cops and they find you here you're going to jail," Frank explained while again maneuvering Josh, this time out the door and straight to one of the divorce attorney's offices.

Josh knew, and respected, the fact Violet had served her country in the Army. He had no idea she should have been classified as a secret agent man assassin.

Violet's ability to set off one legal bombshell after another, effectively blowing up Josh's whole life, would have been astounding if it wasn't so thoroughly terrifying.

Frank and Josh visited six divorce attorneys in rapid succession. Each told them the same as the esteemed Mr. Earnest said "Mr. Bennett, I had a consultation with your wife two days ago. It would be a conflict of interest for me to now represent you."

Violet had gone lawyer shopping.

Even though she had no intention of hiring any of the dozen good or even just-ok, attorneys in the area she'd met with them all, creating a conflict everywhere Josh turned and making it impossible for him to get decent representation on such short order.

For herself, Violet had snapped up the biggest ball-busting, man-hating, divorce attorney in town, Gloria Blanca, and left Josh with nothing but the dregs to choose from. Gloria Blanca wasn't just a man hater, she was a Womens Rights Activist... the bad kind that lived only for the purpose of destroying the Male gender and persona violently at all costs, regardless of the current state and profess of Women's rights. She was still on the warpath, because, well, nobody took the time to tell her she doesn't need to be at war with men any longer. Modern generations understand equality. Gloria Blanca didn't care, she wanted to over-correct the removal of men from society. Gloria was so blatant about her activism, she was a household name from the media and well known in the women's rights activist circles.

Josh ended up with a Mr. John Whitely, Esquire who smelled of cheap booze and bad decisions "No worries, my boy! We'll have this little filly in hand, soon."

Josh went through his litany of questions about divorce, alimony, child support for a kid who wasn't his, paternity, what to do about his home, his bank account, his credit cards, and the protective order.

Whitely assured him "Josh I know this seems like a lot. But you know how to eat an elephant?? Heh??" Josh returned Whitely's words with a blank stare "One bite at a time of course! Leave it to me. First, protective order court 9a.m. tomorrow. Let's get rid of that pesky thing and move forward. Good?"

"Yes, yes" Josh nodded "That will be very good."

Unfortunately, Whitely was tardy, clearly hungover in court and his dismal reputation preceded him. Poor Whitely was on the last legs of alcoholism and didn't really have any other reason to live. No wife, no kids, no pets, no family. He was drinking himself to death and he didn't care.

"Thank you for joining us, Mr. Whitely, at," the judge scowled, checking the courtroom clock "at 9:22 a.m." This man hating judge had seen Whitely's shit before and he was quite frankly tired of it.

"No problem, Judge!" the idiot had no idea the judge was already pissed he was late. That anger was about to be directed at Josh. It never made any logical sense as to why both male and female judges hated men and dad's in the courtroom. Likely a leftover from the dead-beat dad generations of yesteryear. But times have changed and roles have shifted. In the current era, men and fathers were the good people, and the women were turning out in droves to be the bad people in the courtroom and in life.

Violet showed up alone, a trembling flower, acting

completely distraught. How strange it is to see this petite little flower completely "dip-switch" into an award winning actress.

The judge handled her with kid gloves "Mrs. Bennett could you tell me why you want a protective order? Are you afraid of... him." the judge gestured to the opposite side of the courtroom from Violet toward Josh. A look of contempt already set on his face.

"Yes, terribly terrified your honor!" Violet replied.

"And," the judge continued, apparently having decided he'd be Violet's counsel, "you say here in your filing Mr. Bennett has been stalking you, made threats toward you and the little baby girl as well as physically abused you during your marriage?"

Violet was nodding, dabbing a tear from time to time when Josh jumped up with a roar "NO your honor she's lying! I never hurt her not ONCE! The kid isn't even mine!

I'm not stalking her I haven't seen her in a week, please this is stupid!"

The judge arched his white eyebrows until they nearly touched his receding hairline and spat "Stupid?! You find me and my court STUPID young man?!"

"No," Josh muttered "No sir, I mean what Violet is saying about me, where's the proof? I haven't done anything wrong except marrying the wrong woman!" This is a bad dream, this can't be happened Josh thought.

On cue, Violet shrank away from Josh as though he could bash in her head at any moment even though they were separated by a large courtroom and two deputies, and a podium.

Whitely had discovered something fascinating on his tie and seemed to be trying to figure out which spilled cocktail it was. His attention then moved to a tiny knat flying around his smelly body and started waving at it whimsically, when the judge banged his gavel "I have seen and heard enough. I'm granting a six-month protective order. Mrs. Bennett that should be enough time to get the divorce and custody issues mostly resolved then we'll take up this matter, again." Sometimes judges don't even give a shit, they just want to make a ruling to help the parties move forward, even if it is in the wrong direction.

Josh couldn't help himself "Is this some kind of sick joke? What custody? The kid isn't mine!"

Whitely finally clued into the fact his client was about to be put into metal bracelets and stood up just in time to get Josh to sit down and shut up.

The judge let Violet leave first, escorted by the two deputies. Apparently to protect her from her crazy husband.

Later that evening, driving around town aimlessly Josh kept glancing at the four boxes in his back seat. All of his worldly possessions.

"Hey pal," one of the deputies said when it was Josh's turn to leave the courtroom "come with me."

"Here." as though the deputy was explaining everything.

Four boxes, some of Josh's belongings Violet had packed and brought to the courthouse with her that morning to have law enforcement hand off to her soon-to-be-ex.

The top of each box was decorated with a silk rose bouquet.

"She's too good for you, bub. You just leave her alone." the deputy said as he watched Josh stack the boxes and move on. Josh just then realized that anything with a penis is going to automatically take sides with this shitty person called Violet, because well, they have a penis and they secretly see themselves fucking her. Violet learned this early in life and has used it to her advantage since. She knew other men would see her and instantly want to fuck her and she let this passive little mean trick play against Josh. She didn't have to do anything to make it happen, it was a beautiful little weapon. All she had to do was show up, and men would defend her. Little did they know.

Josh realized he really did appear volatile and probably crazy in court today while Violet played the perfect victim seemingly in control of herself and perfectly sane. Josh realized that to be the good guy in court, you simply had to "put on a good show" for the judge, regardless. It worked for a piece of shit like Violet, and he just didn't know this secret yet. Lawyers know it, judges fall for it, day in and day out in family courts across the nation. It has nothing to do with Truth or Reality.

Josh would have to tuck his crazy in if he had any hopes of getting his life back.

But the hits just kept coming. Within that month the county prosecutor was considering two criminal charges against Josh for violating the protective order. Violet knew how to play that card.

It seemed like whenever he turned around Violet was there, acting surprised then shouting for the police.

Insult to injury, Violet had filed false reports to the department of child services against Josh. Josh hasn't seen the baby since he left them in his home. How could he be a danger to the kid? Bitches be doing this to ex baby daddies all over the nation, it's almost expected as normal behavior for the mommas to play this card and no-body is talking about how wrong it is. Shit, the schools do it, the churches do it, instantly taking the side of the mother as if the man is somehow always the bad guy. This bullshit happens daily.

In the jail cell after the second arrest, while waiting for

his poor mom to bail him out, yet again a chatty ex-con asked Josh about his current woes. When Josh explained to the chatty con who then said, "Oh, she's got you on a tracking device fo sho my man."

"A what?" Josh couldn't wrap his mind around it.

"Ya know," chatty continued "there's a little GPS tracker attached, probably to the undercarriage of your car, so wherever you go she can go and pretend you followed HER there. Bitches be crazy dude. You can't tell the sane ones from the crazy ones theze dayz."

As soon as Josh's mom sprung him he drove to "Down Low Digital" which boasted the largest selection of spy grade equipment in the whole Raleigh-Durham area.

"I need you to look at my car, sweep it, whatever you do to find a bug, a plant, a... device thing," said Josh. In a panic to confirm what a criminal had just told him.

"Sure, sure, keep your shirt on. Yeah, I can sweep the car for a device, $50." said the guy wearing the green "Down Low Digital" visor. The bald spot on top shining merrily in the store's flashing display lights.

Josh sighed "Man, I have $100 to my name, my gas tank is on empty and my crazy ex is trying to put me in jail. A little help?"

Donny "Down Low Digital" considered it all and said "I cannot waive the fee but I can tell you right now, you pay me the $50 and I find a device and it turns out to be one of ours, I can't tell you about it. Company policy."

As he walked away, Josh could only grasp his skull like his brains were about to explode out of it. Josh realized that Violet had probably been there already and used her "little trick" of getting free stuff and services by shaking her tits and ass.

That's the moment Josh decided he needed to live off the

grid for a while.

That's when his granddad's boggy patch of land occurred to him and he felt he'd finally found a respite. So, he didn't even notice Violet parked in the adjoining lot with baby Rose attached to her breast and a crooked smile on her face. This bitch really a new kind of evil, or was she? This breed is starting to be the mainstay of the family court system. Somehow if there is karma, this needs to stop.

The legal fees, the court costs, the counter custody/paternity case, Violet was sucking Josh completely dry.

Josh tried many times to find the tracking device himself. Finding nothing he thought maybe a criminal in jail gave him some bad intel. What's this world coming to?

Then, one evening Josh rolled in from another disastrous day in court. His rickety front gate was missing from his grandfather's property. "Did it blow away?" Josh wondered aloud as he scoped the area.

"Fuck." Josh turned and walked up to the lean-to structure. Wanting only to get a few hours of sleep. His shame was so deep he wouldn't hear of his mother or Frank taking him in until he could cut Violet completely out of their lives, roots and all.

Josh ducked to enter the small space and he froze. He looked down to one single head of a Knock Out rosebud ground into the dirt.

Josh dialed 911 feeling both sick and elated "Yes, I need the police out to my place. It's my ex-wife, my almost ex. She's been on my property, stealing and destroying my property!"

The officer who responded looked less than intrigued by Josh's crime of the century and laughed right in Josh's face when Josh told him "Look she even took the gate."

"What's that right there?" asked the officer.

"That's," Josh must have turned white. "Those are my credit cards and my watch. And wedding band." Also ground into the dirt. Not only was Violet pure evil, she had an angry side to her that showed in her remnants of fits of anger she was starting to leave behind.

The officer was done with Josh and got back onto his radio "Yeah, Melba, I'm back in service. Apparently, this guy's wife stole some flowers and a rusty gate but decided not to take the cards and jewelry, or something. The officer had a sarcastic tone of voice such that the dispatcher intuitively understand that they were to treat Josh as a criminal that was simply making up another bogus story." The officer and dispatcher shared a good laugh and Josh could see he would never, ever, get his life back. When you have the power of the pussy on your side like Violet did, there's a mountainous climb out of the underworld, as Josh was beginning to see.

The shitty watch was worth as much as his granddaddy's

bog and if Violet had her way it's also where he'd be buried.

And didn't Violet always get her way?

This story plays out in courtrooms daily across the nation. It's a festering pit of vipers where only Judges and Lawyers win.

Because Violet was able to wage the "Perception" war against Josh, this is how he got fucked.

The judge awarded Violet full custody of Rose, but that only made sense to Josh because IT WASN'T HIS BABY in the first place.

Violet was awarded both real estate properties, figuring she could turn the swampland into condo's. She already took all of Josh's posessions, and because Josh didn't know any better, she got to keep what was in her possession at the judges ruling, including the new Range Rover he paid cash for.

Josh was court ordered to pay $5000 a month in alimony and $1200 a month in child support to Violet. The only way to get that modified was to prove that the kid wasn't his. He already owed his drunken lawyer thousands, and to fight that battle was almost not worth it, but he had to do what was right. Josh couldn't afford to live on his own. He eventually started living out of his car, with barely enough money to eat, he lost a ton of weight and the depression took the rest until Mother Mary found him and brought him home. Josh spent the next few years spending all of his extra change on Lawyers and the legal system to try to get the child support removed and to try and lower the alimony. Josh was financially and mentally ass raped, and knew now why so many divorced dad's take their own lives. There is nothing left for them. Violet took everything, and now she is turning that into multi-millions.

More stories from the

· MORE STORIES FROM THE ·

www.ingramcontent.com/pod-product-compliance
Lightning Source LLC
Chambersburg PA
CBHW071926290426
44110CB00013B/1487